W9-ALN-510

GASB STATEMENT 34 UPDATE
Craig D. Shoulders
Virginia Polytechnic Institute and State University

ADVANCED ACCOUNTING

Seventh Edition

Floyd A. Beams
John A. Brozovsky
Craig D. Shoulders

Prentice
Hall

Upper Saddle River, New Jersey 07458

Acquisitions Editor: *Annie Todd*
Associate editor: *Kathryn Sheehan*
Project editor: *Theresa Festa*
Manufacturer: *Victor Graphics, Inc.*

© 2000 by Prentice Hall, Inc.
Upper Saddle River, New Jersey 07458

All rights reserved. No part of this book may be
reproduced, in any form or by any means,
without permission in writing from the publisher.

Printed in the United States of America

10 9 8 7 6 5 4 3 2

ISBN 0-13-088845-1

Prentice-Hall International (UK) Limited, *London*
Prentice-Hall of Australia Pty. Limited, *Sydney*
Prentice-Hall Canada Inc., *Toronto*
Prentice-Hall Hispanoamericana, S.A., *Mexico*
Prentice-Hall of India Private Limited, *New Delhi*
Prentice-Hall of Japan, Inc., *Tokyo*
Prentice-Hall (Singapore) Pte Ltd
Editora Prentice-Hall do Brasil, Ltda., *Rio de Janeiro*

GASB STATEMENT 34 UPDATE: THE NEW GOVERNMENT REPORTING MODEL

The GASB issued Statement 34, "Basic Financial Statements--and Management's Discussion and Analysis--for State and Local Governments," in June 1999. Statement 34 replaces the general purpose financial statements (discussed on pages 789 to 798 of the text) with an integrated set of fund-based and government-wide financial statements. The statement also requires presentation of management's discussion and analysis as required supplementary information and changes several other significant aspects of government accounting and financial reporting.

Instead of the combined financial statements required currently, the basic financial statements required by Statement 34 include the following eight fund-based financial statements and two government-wide financial statements:

Fund-based statements:
a. *Governmental Funds*
    1. Statement of net assets (balance sheet)
    2. Statement of revenues, expenditures, and changes in fund balances
    3. General fund and major special revenue funds statement of revenues, expenditures, and changes in fund balances--budget and actual (Alternatively, the budget comparison may be presented as required supplementary information instead)
b. *Proprietary Funds*
    1. Statement of net assets (balance sheet)
    2. Statement of revenues, expenses, and changes in net assets
    3. Statement of cash flows (direct method required)
c. *Fiduciary Funds and Fiduciary Component Units*
    1. Statement of net assets (balance sheet)
    2. Statement of changes in net assets

Government-wide financial statements:
a. Government-wide statement of net assets
b. Government-wide statement of activities

The fund-based financial statements are very similar to the current general purpose financial statements (GPFS). Major differences are that (a) the statements report on major governmental funds and major enterprise funds, rather than on governmental fund types and the enterprise fund type, (b) governmental funds, proprietary funds, and fiduciary funds are reported using three separate balance sheets instead of a single combined balance sheet, and (c) general fixed assets, general long-term debt, and discretely presented component units (unless fiduciary in nature) are not reported in fund-based financial statements.

The government-wide financial statements are new. These statements are used to report governmental activities, business-type activities, the primary government totals, and discretely presented component units. All data in the government-wide statements are presented on the flow of economic resources measurement focus (revenue and expense) and accrual basis--even for governmental activities. Fiduciary funds and fiduciary component units are not included in these statements.

Illustrative Financial Statements

The basic formats and content of the financial statements are illustrated in Exhibits 1 to 4. The key features of each of these statements and their contents are noted as we review the statements.

Governmental Fund Statements

The governmental fund statements are illustrated briefly in Exhibit 1. Modified accrual accounting (revenues and expenditures for current financial resources) is used in the governmental funds. This basis of accounting is discussed on pages 730 to 733 of the text and further explained and illustrated throughout Chapter 19 and the first part of Chapter 20.

Several points are worth noting with respect to the **governmental funds balance sheet** in Exhibit 1. First, a separate balance sheet is presented for governmental funds. These are not combined with proprietary and fiduciary funds as in the current GPFS. Significantly, the balance sheet includes a separate column for each major governmental fund and a column with aggregated information for all other governmental funds as well as a total column for all governmental funds--instead of a separate column for each governmental fund type.

Major fund reporting is a significant contribution of Statement 34. Using this approach, the basic financial statements provide specific fund information on each of the most significant funds of a government. The general fund is always a major fund. Other funds must be reported as major funds if they meet both of the following criteria:

a. Total assets, liabilities, revenues, or expenditures/expenses (excluding extraordinary items) of that individual governmental or enterprise fund are at least *10 percent* of the *corresponding* total (assets, liabilities, and so forth) for *all* funds of that *category or type* (that is, total governmental or total enterprise funds), *and*

b. Total assets, liabilities, revenues, or expenditures/expenses (excluding extraordinary items) of the individual governmental fund or enterprise fund are at least *5 percent* of the *corresponding* total for *all* governmental *and* enterprise funds *combined*.

All governmental funds that are not major funds are aggregated in a single column in the fund-based statements. A combining statement(s) must be presented in the CAFR to support this "Other governmental funds" column.

The **governmental fund statement of revenues, expenditures, and changes in fund balances** in Exhibit 1 is similar to the balance sheet in that major fund reporting is required. The accounts reported and the reporting format of the statement are the same as for the most common approach to presenting this statement under current GAAP (Exhibit 19-8, page 746) until "Other financing sources (uses)." Several points should be noted after that:

a. Statement 34 eliminates the distinction between operating transfers and residual equity transfers. All transfers are reported as other financing sources and uses.

Exhibit 1 Governmental Fund Financial Statements

	General Fund	Major Fund #1	Major Fund #2	Major Fund #N	Other Governmental Funds	Total
Governmental Fund Balance Sheet						
Assets (list)						
Liabilities (list)	Current Financial Resources Measurement Focus and Modified Accrual Basis (Revenues and Expenditures)					
Fund Balance						

	General Fund	Major Fund #1	Major Fund #2	Major Fund #N	Other Governmental Funds	Total
Governmental Fund Operating Statement						
Revenues (list)						
Expenditures (list)						
Excess of revenues over expenditures						
Other financing sources (uses) (list) Includes all transfers	Current Financial Resources Measurement Focus and Modified Accrual Basis (Revenues and Expenditures)					
Special items						
Net change in fund balance before extraordinary items						
Extraordinary items						
Net change in fund balance						
Fund balance--beginning						
Fund balance--ending						

A statement of revenues, expenditures, and changes in fund balances--budget and actual (on the budgetary basis) is required for the General Fund and for each major Special Revenue Fund with a legally adopted annual budget. This budgetary comparison statement may be presented as a basic financial statement or as required supplementary information. It is not illustrated here.

b. **Special items,** if any, are reported after other financing sources (uses). Special items is a new reporting classification required by Statement 34, which defines special items as arising from significant transactions or other events that are (1) *within the control of management* and (2) *either* unusual in nature *or* infrequent in occurrence. Sale of a major general fixed asset could be an example of a special item.

c. Net change in fund balance before extraordinary items is reported. Then, any extraordinary items affecting governmental funds are reported.

d. The final subtotal is net change in fund balances.

A **budgetary comparison statement** is required as part of the basic financial statements only for the General Fund and for each major special revenue fund. Additionally, this statement may be presented as required supplementary information instead of as a basic financial statement. The statement must (1) be presented using the budgetary basis of accounting and (2) include a column presenting the original budget in addition to the columns required prior to Statement 34. Hence, the statement of revenues, expenditures, and changes in fund balances-- budget and actual typically will have the following column headings:

Original Budget	Revised Budget	Actual (on budgetary basis)	Variance

Proprietary Fund Statements

The required proprietary fund statements--balance sheet, statement of revenues, expenses, and changes in fund equity, and statement of cash flows--are illustrated in Exhibit 2. Accrual accounting on the flow of economic resources (revenues and expenses) measurement focus is used for proprietary funds.

The primary differences between the **proprietary funds balance sheet** under Statement 34 (Exhibit 2) and the combined statements required under current GAAP include:

a. Presentation of a separate balance sheet for proprietary funds.

b. The statements include a separate column for each major enterprise fund and a column with aggregate information for all other enterprise funds, as well as a total enterprise funds column for the fund type instead of only a column for the enterprise fund type. (Note that major fund reporting is not used for internal service funds, only a single column for the fund type is presented.)

c. The enterprise fund definition is changed by Statement 34. Under Statement 34, enterprise funds *may* be used to report *any* activity for which a *fee* is *charged* to external users for goods or services. Such activities are *required* to be reported as enterprise funds *if any* one of the following *criteria* is *met*.

   1. The activity is financed with debt that is secured solely by a pledge of the net revenues from fees and charges of the activity.

Exhibit 2 Proprietary Fund Financial Statements

Proprietary Fund Balance Sheet						
	Major Enterprise Fund #1	Major Enterprise Fund #2	Major Enterprise Fund #N	Other EFs	Total Enterprise Funds	Internal Service Funds
Assets (list)	**Economic Resources Measurement Focus and Accrual Basis (Revenues & Expenses)**					
Liabilities (list)						
Net Assets: Invested in capital assets, net of related debt Restricted net assets Unrestricted net assets						

Proprietary Fund Operating Statement						
	Major Enterprise Fund #1	Major Enterprise Fund #2	Major Enterprise Fund #N	Other Enterprise Funds	Total Enterprise Funds	Internal Service Funds
Operating revenues (detailed)	**Economic Resources Measurement Focus and Accrual Basis (Revenues & Expenses)**					
Operating expenses (detailed)						
Operating income						
Nonoperating revenues and expenses (detailed)						
Income before other revenues, expenses, and transfers						
Capital contributions (grant, developer, and other), additions to permanent and term endowments, special and extraordinary items (detailed), and transfers						
Increase (decrease) in net assets						
Net assets/fund equity—beginning						
Net assets/fund equity—ending						

Exhibit 2 continued Proprietary Fund Financial Statements

	Major Enterprise Fund #1	Major Enterprise Fund #2	Major Enterprise Fund #N	Other Enterprise Funds	Total Enterprise Funds	Internal Service Funds
Proprietary Fund Statement of Cash Flows						
Cash flows from **operating activities** *Direct method required* (Detailed)						
Cash flows from **noncapital financing activities** (Detailed)						
Cash flows from **capital and related financing activities** (Detailed)						
Cash flows from **investing activities** (Detailed)						
Net increase (decrease) in cash						
Cash--beginning Cash--ending						

2. Laws or regulations require that the activity's costs of providing services, including capital costs (such as depreciation or debt service), be recovered with fees and charges rather than with taxes or similar revenues.
3. The pricing policies of the activity establish fees and charges designed to recover its costs, including capital costs (such as depreciation or debt service).

d. Fund equity (which may be called net assets) is not classified as contributed capital and retained earnings. New classifications are required as shown in the statement. These classifications are:

1. **Invested in capital (fixed) assets, net of related debt,** which equals the fixed assets of the fund less all fixed asset-related debt (whether current or long-term).
2. **Restricted net assets**, or restricted equity, equals the difference between (1) assets externally restricted by creditors (perhaps through debt covenants), grantors, donors, or laws and regulations of other governments, or internally by constitutional provisions or enabling legislation and (2) liabilities payable from those restricted assets. The restrictions must be more narrow than the purposes of the fund being reported.
3. **Unrestricted net assets** is the difference between the remaining assets and liabilities of the fund. Restricted net assets must be reclassified as unrestricted when the government satisfies the restriction.

The proprietary funds **statement of revenues, expenses, and changes in fund equity** in Exhibit 2 differs from the combined statement of revenues, expenses, and changes in fund equity or retained earnings (see page 797) required before Statement 34 in several ways. First, like the

6

proprietary funds balance sheet, the operating statement focuses on major Enterprise Funds and on the Internal Service Fund type rather than just on the fund types.

Another difference from the pre-Statement 34 combined operating statement for proprietary funds is that items reported after nonoperating revenues and expenses are not distinguished between transactions affecting income and retained earnings and those affecting contributed capital. Indeed, contributed capital and retained earnings classifications are not used under Statement 34 guidelines. Also, note that no net income number is reported. The GASB has adopted what it refers to as a comprehensive income approach and does not attempt to identify net income.

Finally, capital grants (and other capital contributions), special items, extraordinary items, and transfers are all reported after "Income before other revenues, expenses, and transfers" and before "Increase (Decrease) in net assets." Transfers are no longer classified as operating versus residual equity transfers. All transfers, including payments in lieu of taxes, are simply reported as transfers. Operating grants continue to be reported as nonoperating revenues.

The **proprietary funds statement of cash flows** in Exhibit 2 differs from the combined statement of cash flows required before Statement 34 in two primary ways. First, the statement focuses on major Enterprise Funds and on the Internal Service Fund type rather than just on the fund types. Second, the *direct method* of presenting cash flows from operating activities is *required* by Statement 34. Both the direct and indirect methods were permissible before Statement 34.

Fiduciary Fund Statements

Fiduciary fund reporting and the definition and nature of fiduciary funds are changed significantly by Statement 34. Fiduciary fund reporting is by fund type, as was true before Statement 34, but the definition and types of fiduciary funds is changed by Statement 34. As seen in Exhibit 3, the fiduciary fund types under Statement 34 are:

a. Pension trust funds--Same as previously
b. Private-purpose trust funds--Resources held in trust for the *benefit of parties that are not part of the government* rather than for government programs.
c. Investment trust fund--Same as previously, that is, to account for the external portion of investment pools.
d. Agency funds--Used to account only for resources held as an *agent for parties outside the government.* Agency fund resources cannot be held for other funds.

Note that fiduciary funds are used to report only resources held for the benefit of parties other than the reporting government.

Most expendable and nonexpendable trust funds under the pre-Statement 34 guidance are to be reported as special revenue funds and permanent funds, respectively, under Statement 34. (Permanent Funds is a new governmental fund type which should be used to account for resources that "are legally restricted to the extent that only earnings, and not principal, may be

Figure 3   Fiduciary Fund Financial Statements

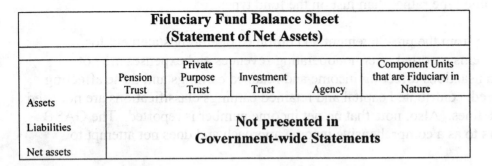

	Pension Trust	Private Purpose Trust	Investment Trust	Agency	Component Units that are Fiduciary in Nature
Fiduciary Fund Balance Sheet					
(Statement of Net Assets)					
Assets					
Liabilities		**Not presented in Government-wide Statements**			
Net assets					

	Pension Trust	Private Purpose Trust	Investment Trust	Component Units that are Fiduciary in Nature
Fiduciary Fund and Fiduciary Component Units				
Statement of Changes in Net Assets				
Additions (Detailed)		**Not presented in Government-wide Statements**		
Deductions (Detailed)				
Net increase (decrease)				
Net assets--beginning				
Net assets--ending				

used for purposes that support the reporting government's programs--that is, for the benefit of the government or its citizenry."

The required fiduciary fund financial statements are the *statement of fiduciary fund net assets* and the *statement of changes in fiduciary fund net assets*. These statements are essentially the same as those of pension trust funds. Fiduciary funds and fiduciary component units are reported only in the fund-based statements--they are not reported in the government-wide statements.

Government-wide Statements

The two required government-wide statements are the statement of net assets and the statement of activities. These statements are presented using essentially the same measurement focus and basis of accounting as proprietary funds--the flow of economic resources measurement focus and the accrual basis of accounting. These statements distinctly report information on governmental activities and business-type activities as well as on the primary government and on non-fiduciary discretely presented component units.

In reviewing these government-wide financial statements in Exhibits 4 and 5, recognize that governmental activities include all governmental fund assets and liabilities, general fixed assets (including infrastructure and net of accumulated depreciation), general long-term debt (using the effective interest method), and the assets and liabilities of internal service activities that provide the majority of their services to general government departments. The information is aggregated. Appropriate eliminations and adjustments are made to convert the data to the revenues and expenses basis required to be used in the government-wide financial statements. Business-type activities include enterprise fund activities and any internal service activities that provide a majority of their services to enterprise activities. For some governments, this will simply be the same data reported in the total enterprise funds column of their proprietary funds balance sheet.

Note also several other aspects of the **government-wide statement of net assets**. First, current and noncurrent liabilities are distinguished. The governmental activities column includes general long-term debt (measured using the revenue and expense based approach of proprietary funds). Second, the net assets are classified in the same three categories used for proprietary activities. Next, note that interfund payables and receivables between funds used to account for governmental activities are eliminated. Likewise, interfund payables and receivables between funds used to account for business-type activities are eliminated. Payables and receivables between governmental activities and business-type activities are reflected in the asset section of the governmental activities column and the business-type activities column as internal balances. The primary government total is presented after eliminating the internal balances. Finally, notice that discretely presented component units (other than those that are fiduciary in nature) are presented in the government-wide statements. They are not included in the fund-based statements.

The format of the **government-wide statement of activities**—the most unique of the new statements—is illustrated in Exhibit 5. This statement should be viewed as having two distinct parts. The upper portion of the statement focuses on cost of services and reports both the total expenses and the net expenses of the government by function. It is based on the formula:

Expenses – Program revenues = Net (Expenses) Revenues

The lower portion of the statement intends to report how the net program expenses incurred during the year compared with general revenues. It reports various types of general revenues, contributions to Permanent funds, special items, extraordinary items, and transfers.

Observe in reviewing the government-wide statement of activities in Exhibit 5 that governmental activities and business-type activities are distinguished both in the presentation of functional classifications (the rows) and in the presentation of net expenses (revenues) and changes in net assets (the columns). The primary government and discretely presented component units are distinguished in similar fashion.

Exhibit 4 Government-wide Statement of Net Assets

	Governmental Activities	Business-type Activities	Primary Government (total)	Component Units (that are not Fiduciary in nature)
Government-wide Balance Sheet				
Assets:				
Cash	XX	XX	XX	XX
.				
.				
.				
Internal balances	(XX)	XX		
Capital assets (including general fixed assets, including infrastructure, and net of accumulated depreciation)	XX	XX	XX	XX
	XX	XX	XX	XX
Liabilities:				
Current liabilities	XX	XX	XX	XX
Noncurrent liabilities (including general long-term debt presented using the proprietary fund approach)	XX	XX	XX	XX
	XX	XX	XX	XX
Net assets:				
Invested in capital assets, net of related debt	XX	XX	XX	XX
Restricted net assets	XX	XX	XX	XX
Unrestricted net assets	XX	XX	XX	XX
	XX	XX	XX	XX

Exhibit 5   Statement of Activities Format

| Functions | Expenses | Program Revenues | | | Net (Expense) Revenue and Changes in Net Assets | | | |
| | | Charges for Services | Operating Grants and Contributions | Capital Grants and Contributions | Primary Government | | | Component Units |
					Governmental Activities	Business-type Activities	Total	
Primary government								
Governmental activities								
Function # 1	XXX	XX	X	X	(XX)	—	(XX)	—
Function # 2	XXX	XX	X	—	(XX)	—	(XX)	—
Function # 3	XXX	XX	X	X	(X)	—	(X)	—
Total governmental activities	XXXX	XXX	XX	XX	(XX)	—	(XX)	—
Business-type activities (BTA)								
BTA # 1	XXXX	XXXX	—	X	XX	XX	XX	—
BTA # 2	XXXXX	XXXX	—	XX	—	XXX	XXX	—
Total business-type activities	XXXXXX	XXXX	—	XX	—	XXX	XXX	—
Total primary government	XXXXXX	XXXXX	XX	XXX	(XXX)	XXX	XX	—
Component units (CUs)								
CU # 1	XXXX	XXXX	XX	XX	—	—	—	XX
General revenues—detailed					XXX	X	XX	XX
Contributions to permanent funds					XX	—	XX	—
Special items					X	—	X	—
Transfers					XX	(XX)	—	—
Total general revenues, contributions, special items, and transfers					XXX	X	XXX	XX
Change in net assets					X	XX	XX	XX
Net assets—beginning					XXXXX	XXXXX	XXXX	XXXXX
Net assets—ending					XXXXX	XXXXX	XXXX	XXXXX

Source: GASB Statement 34, para. 54.

Program revenues raised for a function are deducted from the expenses incurred for the function to derive the net (expenses) revenues of that function. Program revenues are described as revenues derived "directly from the program itself or from parties outside the reporting government's constituency." Program revenues include:

a. Charges to users for services provided
b. Operating grants and contributions that are restricted to use for activities classified in a particular function but not restricted solely to capital asset construction, acquisition, or improvement.
c. Capital grants and contributions that are restricted to use for activities classified in a particular function and restricted *solely to capital asset* construction, acquisition, or improvement.
d. Investment income that is legally or contractually restricted to use for a particular program.

Under Statement 34, all other revenues are general revenues. *All taxes*, even if restricted to a specific program, *are general revenues*. Grants and investment income that do not meet the requirements to be reported as program revenues are among the general revenues. Contributions to endowments, special items, extraordinary items, and transfers are reported separate from and following general revenues.

Recognize that the amount reported as a special item or extraordinary item in the statement of activities typically will differ from the amount reported in the governmental funds statements because different measurement focuses are used in the two statements. Also note that the statement is not intended to report net income, and no net income number is presented. The final subtotal is simply net change in net assets.

The illustration used here presents only one column for expenses, which presumes that indirect costs such as those normally reported under the general government function have not been allocated. Alternatively, governments may choose not to report a general government function and allocate those costs to the other functional categories. If so, a second column showing the allocation of those indirect costs is required. Depreciation on general fixed assets, including infrastructure fixed assets, should be allocated to functions. Interest on general long-term debt incurred for the benefit of a particular function should be reported as expenses of that function. Any other interest on general long-term debt should be reported as a separate line item.

Required Reconciliations

Governments are required to present a reconciliation between the governmental funds statements and the governmental activities column of the government-wide statements. Likewise, a reconciliation of the enterprise fund total columns from the enterprise fund statements (except the cash flow statement) and the business-type activities column in the government-wide statements must be prepared. The reconciliation may be presented either (1) on the face of the fund-based statements or (2) as separate schedules. Though not illustrated here, the concept is the same as the reconciliations required by current GAAP in a statement of cash flows or between the GAAP-basis statement of revenues, expenditures, and changes in fund balances and the budgetary comparison statement.

Management's Discussion and Analysis

Another new requirement of Statement 34 is the presentation of a management's discussion and analysis letter as required supplementary information *preceding* the financial statements. The GASB prescribes a detailed list of issues and information that must be covered in the MD&A, which is essentially a highly structured letter of transmittal. It is important to note that the MD&A:

    a. is not a forecast.
    b. is based on currently known facts, decisions, or conditions.
    c. introduces the government's basic financial statements.
    d. provides an analytical overview of the government's activities.

The issues required to be addressed in MD&A are outlined in Exhibit 6.

Other Issues

Three other specific issues are worthy of particular attention in the context of the new reporting model. The options for the treatment of infrastructure fixed assets, the new classifications of interfund transactions, and revenue recognition for nonexchange transactions--particularly under the flow of economic resources measurement focus--are three major areas of interest in the new reporting model.

General Government Infrastructure

Because governments have *not* been required to capitalize (or depreciate) general fixed assets infrastructure in the past, the GASB permitted governments the option of doing less than capitalizing and depreciating all infrastructure general fixed assets when they adopt Statement 34. The infrastructure-related options include:

    a. Governments are only *required* to capitalize expenditures for major general government infrastructure fixed assets incurred in fiscal years ending after June 30, 1981.
    b. Governments are permitted to use a modified approach for accounting for infrastructure fixed assets that are part of a network or subsystem of a network that the government:
        1. manages using an asset management system with specified characteristics, and
        2. documents is being preserved approximately at (or above) a target condition level determined by the reporting government.
    c. All expenditures made for infrastructure fixed assets accounted for under the modified approach are charged to expense when incurred. Only additions and improvements to

those assets are capitalized. Depreciation and accumulated depreciation are not reported on those assets.

Interfund Transactions

Most interfund transactions are accounted for and reported in the same manner as before Statement 34 was issued. But, Statement 34 uses different terminology and does change the reporting of transfers and interfund payments in lieu of taxes. The new classifications and their relationships to the previous classifications are:

a. Reciprocal interfund activity includes
   1. Interfund loans--same as before Statement 34
   2. Interfund services provided and used--Same as quasi-external transactions but exclude interfund payments in lieu of taxes
b. Nonreciprocal interfund activity includes
   1. Interfund transfers--includes all transfers and payments in lieu of taxes. Residual equity and operating transfers are not distinguished. All transfers are reported as other financing sources (uses) in the governmental fund statement of revenues, expenditures and changes in fund balances or as the last item before change in net assets in the proprietary fund operating statement and in the government-wide statement of activities.
   2. Interfund reimbursements--same as reimbursement transactions under the old guidance.

Revenue Recognition for Nonexchange Transactions

Revenue recognition in the government-wide financial statements is determined using the flow of economic resources measurement focus and accrual basis (i.e., revenue and expense accounting), rather than the modified accrual basis of accounting. GASB Statement 33, "Accounting and Financial Reporting for Nonexchange Transactions," provides specific guidance for when to recognize revenues from most nonexchange transactions such as taxes, fines, and intergovernmental grants under both the accrual and the modified accrual bases of accounting. While new terminology is introduced in GASB Statement 33, the statement changes little with respect to revenue recognition under the modified accrual basis of accounting for major revenue sources such as property taxes, sales taxes, income taxes, or intergovernmental grants. Revenue recognition on the *accrual basis* is required to follow these guidelines:

- *Derived tax revenues*—taxes such as sales taxes and income taxes that are imposed on exchange transactions generally are to be recognized when the underlying transaction (i.e., sale or earning of income) occurs.
- *Imposed nonexchange transactions other than derived tax revenues*—which include such revenue sources as property taxes and fines are to be recognized as revenues in the earliest period when use of the resources is permitted or required, assuming they

are earned or levied and objectively measurable. For property taxes, this typically means the period for which levied.

- *Government-mandated nonexchange transactions (programs that senior level governments require subordinate governments to perform) and voluntary nonexchange transactions (including most grants and private donations)*—revenues are recognized when all eligibility requirements, including time restrictions, have been met. The primary example of these types of transactions that has been dealt with extensively in the text is "expenditure-driven" grants. Statement 33 requires that revenues from such grants be recognized when the recipient has made allowable expenditures under the grant provisions.

For *modified accrual* revenue recognition, Statement 33 requires that the *availability* criterion--including the "collected by year end or soon enough thereafter to be used to pay the liabilities of the period" criterion--must be met in addition to the above conditions. The availability criterion does *not* apply to accrual basis revenue recognition under the flow of economic resources measurement focus and accrual basis used in the government-wide statements.

Concluding Comments

GASB Statement 34 is the most significant development in government accounting and financial reporting since the 1930s. While still viewed as evolutionary in nature, the standard impacts multiple aspects of government financial reporting from the statements presented to the format of the statements to the reporting of major funds instead of fund types to the portion of the government reported in each statement. It further affects the types of funds used to account for certain types of activities, the classification and reporting of interfund transactions, the treatment of general government infrastructure fixed assets, the basis of accounting used to report general government activities, and many other aspects of government financial accounting and reporting.

The GASB continues to move ahead from the foundation established in Statement 34. Multiple implementation guides are being developed not only for preparers and auditors of government financial statements but also for users of these statements. The GASB has issued Statement 35 requiring government colleges and universities to apply Statement 34 just as all other government entities are required to do.

Exhibit 6: Minimum Requirements for Management's Discussion and Analysis

At a minimum, MD&A should include:

1. A brief discussion of the basic financial statements—including:
   - the relationships of the statements to each other,
   - the differences in the information provided, and
   - analyses that help readers understand why information reported in fund financial statements either (1) reinforces that in the government-wide statements, or (2) provides additional information.

2. Condensed financial information—derived from government-wide statements—comparing the current year to the prior year. At a minimum SLGs should present information necessary to support analysis of financial position and results of operations (required in 3 below), including these elements:
   - Total assets—distinguishing between capital and other assets
   - Total liabilities—distinguishing between long-term debt outstanding and other liabilities
   - Total net assets—distinguishing among amounts invested in capital assets (net of related debt), restricted amounts, and unrestricted amounts
   - Program revenues—by major source
   - General revenues—by major source
   - Total revenues
   - Program expenses—at a minimum by function
   - Total expenses
   - Excess (deficiency) before contributions to term and permanent endowments or permanent fund principal, special and extraordinary items, and transfers
   - Contributions and transfers
   - Special items and extraordinary items
   - Change in net assets
   - Beginning and ending net assets

3. An analysis of the SLG's overall financial position and results of operations—to assist users assess whether financial position has improved or deteriorated as a result of the year's operations.
   - The analysis should address both governmental and business-type activities—as reported in the government-wide statements—and include reasons for significant changes from the prior year.
   - Important economic factors—such as changes in the tax or employment bases—that significantly affected the year's operating results should be discussed.
   - The analysis should include comments about the significant changes in the fund balance or fund equity of individual funds.

Exhibit 6: Minimum Requirements for Management's Discussion and Analysis (Continued)

4.   An analysis of balances and transactions of individual funds. The analysis should address the reasons for significant changes in fund balances or fund net assets and whether restrictions, commitments, or other limitations significantly affect the availability of fund resources for future use.

5.   An analysis of significant variations between (1) original and final budget amounts and (2) final budget amounts and actual budget results for the General Fund (or its equivalent).
Note: The analysis should include any currently known reasons for variations that are expected to have a significant effect on future services or liquidity.

6.   A description of capital asset and long-term debt activity during the year—including a discussion of (1) material commitments for capital expenditures, (2) any changes in credit ratings, and (3) whether debt limitations may affect the financing of planned facilities or services.

7.   Governments that use the modified approach reporting some or all of their infrastructure assets also should discuss:
   - Significant changes in the assessed condition of eligible infrastructure assets from previous condition assessments.
   - How the current assessed condition compares to the condition level at which the government has established and disclosed that it intends to preserve eligible infrastructure assets.
   - Any significant differences between the estimated annual amount to maintain/preserve eligible infrastructure assets compared with the actual amounts spent during the current period.

8.   A description of currently known facts, decisions, or conditions that are expected to have a material effect on financial position (net assets) or results of operations (revenues, expenses, and other changes in net assets).

QUESTIONS
1. What basis (bases) of accounting is used to report governmental activities under Statement 34?
2. Statement 34 changes the definition of Enterprise Funds. What is the new definition? Statement 34 defines fiduciary funds differently than has been true in the past. What is the new definition? Under Statement 34 what type of fund will be used to account for Expendable Trust Fund resources that must be used to help finance a government's adult literacy program?
3. What is meant by "major fund reporting"? How does this differ from reporting by fund type as currently required in general purpose financial statements? For what fund types is major fund reporting required? For what fund types is fund type reporting required?
4. How does a government determine which governmental funds are major funds? How does a government decide which proprietary funds are major?
5. What are the required basic financial statements under Statement 34?
6. What are special items? How are they reported?
7. Distinguish general revenues from program revenues. Provide several examples of each.
8. How are interfund transactions to be classified and reported under GASB Statement 34?

EXERCISES

Exercise 1

1. According to *Statement 34*, what are the required government-wide financial statements?
   a. Statement of Net Assets and Statement of Cash Flows
   b. Statement of Net Assets and Statement of Activities
   c. Statement of Net Assets, Statement of Activities, and Statement of Cash Flows
   d. Statement of Net Assets, Statement of Changes in Net Assets, and Statement of Activities
2. Fund-based financial statements require which type of reporting?
   a. fund type reporting
   b. account group reporting
   c. individual fund reporting
   d. major fund reporting
3. The GASB requires the assets, liabilities and equities of most Internal Service Funds to be reported as part of :
   a. governmental activities in the government-wide statement of net assets
   b. business-type activities in the government-wide statement of net assets
   c. component unit activities in the government-wide statement of net assets
   d. They are not included in the government-wide statements
4. Fiduciary funds and fiduciary component units are reported:
   a. Only in fund-based financial statements
   b. Only in government-wide financial statements
   c. In both fund-based and government-wide financial statements
   d. In neither fund-based nor government-wide financial statements

5. Nonfiduciary, discretely presented component units are presented:
   a. Only in fund-based financial statements

b. Only in government-wide financial statements

c. In both fund-based and government-wide financial statements

d. In neither fund-based nor government-wide financial statements

Exercise 2

1. Some of the significant guidance illustrated in *Statement 34* does not include:
   a. changes in the definition of fiduciary funds and Enterprise funds
   b. changes in the reporting of interfund transfers
   c. creation of another governmental fund type called Permanent funds
   d. requiring residual equity transfers and capital grants to be reported as contributed capital in proprietary fund financial statements

2. Because of the new definition of fiduciary funds, most Expendable Trust Funds will be treated as:
   a. Permanent funds
   b. Enterprise Funds
   c. Special Revenue Funds
   d. Agency Funds

3. An Enterprise fund is permitted to be used to report any activity for which a fee is charged to external users for goods and services. Which of the following is not included as part of the criteria for required Enterprise fund reporting?
   a. Laws or regulations require that the activity's costs of providing services, including capital costs, be recovered with fees and charges rather than with taxes or similar revenues.
   b. The pricing policies of the activity establish fees and charges designed to recover its costs, excluding capital costs.
   c. The activity is financed with debt that is secured solely by a pledge of the net revenues from fees and charges of the activity.
   d. None of the above

4. General-fixed assets and general long-term debt are reported:
   a. Only in fund-based financial statements
   b. Only in government-wide financial statements
   c. In both fund-based and government-wide financial statements
   d. In neither fund-based nor government-wide financial statements

5. Fund-type reporting continues to be required for:
   a. Internal Service funds and Enterprise funds
   b. Fiduciary funds
   c. Enterprise funds and fiduciary funds
   d. Internal Service funds and fiduciary funds

Exercise 3

1. A major fund exists if two criteria are met. Which of the following is not included in the criteria:
   a. Total assets, liabilities, revenues or expenditures/expenses of the individual fund are at least 15% of the corresponding total of assets, liabilities, revenues or expenditures/expenses for all funds of that category or type.
   b. Total assets, liabilities, revenues or expenditures/expenses of the individual fund are at least 5% of the corresponding total of all governmental and enterprise funds combined.
   c. Both are included in the criteria.
   d. Neither is included in the criteria.
2. Nonreciprocal interfund activities include:
   a. interfund transfers
   b. interfund reimbursements
   c. interfund loans
   d. both a and b
   e. All of the above
3. Reciprocal interfund activities include:
   a. interfund transfers
   b. interfund loans
   c. interfund reimbursements
   d. both a and b
   e. All of the above
4. *Payments in lieu of taxes* that are not payments for, and reasonably equivalent in value to, services provided are included in the following category:
   a. Interfund reimbursements
   b. Interfund loan
   c. Interfund services provided and used
   d. Interfund transfers
5. Special items result from significant transactions or other events that are:
   a. both unusual in nature and infrequent in occurrence
   b. within the control of management and either unusual in nature or infrequent in occurrence
   c. both unusual in nature and infrequent in occurrence and not within the control of management
   d. either unusual in nature or infrequent in occurrence

Exercise 4

How should each of these transactions of a general government department be reported (a) in the governmental funds statement of revenues, expenditures, and changes in fund balances and (b) in the government-wide statement of activities? Include the reporting of related amounts such as depreciation and interest.

1. Purchase of equipment with a 5-year life at the beginning of the year for $40,000
2. Issuance of a 3-year, 6%, $100,000 note on January 1
3. Levy of property taxes for the year of $1,000,000. The estimated uncollectible portion of the taxes is $20,000 and $105,000 is not expected to be collected until after the first 60 days of the next fiscal year.
4. Transfer of $200,000 from the General Fund to a Capital Projects Fund
5. Received and earned a restricted operating grant of $120,000